Tailor-Made Mom:

Get the Relationship Between
You and Your Daughter
to Fit

Morenda Wysinger

ISBN-13: 978-0692953426
ISBN-10: 0692953426

Affirmation of the Author

From the moment Morenda knew she had conceived her daughter, she was a great mother, on the road to developing an awesome relationship with her child. She was always a loyal and loving friend, and she was a great mom because she had the essential foundation of parenting...LOVE. The love that she displayed and actively gave to her daughter, even as a young mother, was unparalleled. Morenda made the conscious decision to be Monaye's mother, and she took on the responsibility with her entire heart and soul. I am humbled when my friend now calls me a good mother because, little does she know, I learned a lot from her example.

Devon Berry, mother of actress, Daria Johns

Affirmation of the Author

Morenda's relationship with her daughter is unlike anything I've ever seen. How she has managed to create an authentic bond with not only her own daughter, but also with other young girls and women that she mentors, is mind boggling. I don't believe her relationship with her daughter or her mentees is by chance; it is instead by design.

My mother and I have the most incredible bond that a mother and son can have. I feel extremely blessed to be so connected to the person who brought me into the world, especially when I look at those who have not been granted that gift.

Now, if you are looking to understand your own child or to make a true connection with someone despite an age gap, Morenda is one to study -- an excellent pattern!

David Shands, Founder & CEO of
Sleep is 4 Suckers/Sleepless Knights

About the Author

Chicago native Morenda Wysinger is a woman of purpose. She is the mother of one child, Monaye, who is an honor graduate of Howard University and an educator in Atlanta, Georgia. Morenda & Monaye co-founded Mother and Daughter Enterprise in 2014.

Morenda – a mother at heart, coach, and motivator – lives to impact the lives of young women. She is a mentor, striving to bring out greatness in others and leave a legacy in the earth.

She believes in helping others conquer their challenges and pursue their hopes and dreams – often to the exclusion of her own – facilitating seminars for single parents, youth abstinence, and self-esteem education. Additionally, she co-developed and facilitated a mentoring program for teen girls. Despite or perhaps because Morenda was a teen mother, she has used her life's experience to mold and empower that demographic. This optimist believes she has found her calling in life and that others can benefit from it. She resides in the Albany, Georgia area.

Dedication

To my daughter who esteems me as if I am the greatest mother on the planet and who continues to put forth the effort to maintain a healthy mother-daughter relationship. It is because of you that I'm able to share a piece of our tailor-made relationship with the world. You are a trailblazer who has broken patterns and now sets greater standards for my legacy. I am thankful to God for His trust in me to assist you in that journey and nourish your ambition to excel. No words can express how much I love and need you! You are an inspiration.

To my mother who has partnered with me to prove that it's never too late to build an unbreakable mother-daughter bond. I love you, and I vow to continue to make you proud. To my mentees who give me the privilege of "sewing" some of these tailor-made techniques onto the garments that are their lives, thereby helping them become better young ladies. I believe in you.

Acknowledgements

To God, the One who deserves all the credit for ordering my steps! Even when I didn't understand His logic, He walked with me and assured me that He had a plan. Thank You for giving me the grace and the passion to walk in the authority of who You have purposed me to be -- a mother, a mentor, and a motivator, and now, I can write about it.

Enormous gratitude is due to my "Rocky Balboa", Victor Powell. You are the epitome of what a true fighter looks like. It is because of you that I can't stop and won't stop when life throws me a blow. Thank you for perfecting my punch to get this book published.

Special thanks to my mentee -- Ke'Cia Griffin – who I believe God sent into my life as an Angel. I appreciate your selflessness. Thank you for always putting forth effort and taking risks even when you don't think you're good enough. My book cover looks amazing! A. Pearl Brown, thank you for taking time out of your busy schedule to edit my book. You always partner with me gracefully to produce great things and people. I honor and love you PNC.

Table of Contents

Introduction

As I was preparing for a major event, I found the most beautiful black dress at a boutique. It defined my personality and style so well. There was only one problem…it did not fit and flatter me. Still excited about this dress, I decided to purchase it and take it to my tailor. I knew the dress needed more than minor alterations, and in fact, it needed some serious work done to it for it to look as if it had been specifically made for me. When I arrived at my tailor's shop, I anxiously expressed my concerns and told him that I would be departing for Chicago soon and that I needed the dress to wear for a special occasion. He asked me to put the dress on so he could see what needed to be done. When I came out of the fitting room, he admired the dress and said, "This is going to take some work, but no worries. Let's work together to get it to fit exactly how it should on you."

You see, when your clothes do not fit properly, it's possible for them to look as if you are wearing hand-me-downs. Similarly, your relationship with your daughter should fit well, not like the two of you do not belong together. Fortunately, he was willing to use a few tools and techniques to get the dress to fit. On my visit to Theo the Tailor, I had an epiphany.

We'll use the tailoring analogy and a few tailoring tools and techniques to take the journey toward becoming a successful shaper of your mother-daughter relationships. Hopefully, you will laugh, say a few "uh huhs" in agreement because of your experiences, and be inspired to get your mother-daughter relationship to fit or fit better.

The relationship that my daughter and I share has helped many people, so I was inspired by them and others to write this book. Allow me to share my experience and guidance with you so that you can have a tailor-made relationship with your daughters.

Chapter

ONE

You

Made this Purchase.
Own and Value It!

That special dress that you bought did not just jump off a rack and onto the counter, nor did it pay for itself. Think about how we were all created. We did not just end up on Earth without someone making a decision. No matter how your daughter was conceived, she did not choose you...just as the dress did not insist you purchase it. So, if you can remember this one thing, it will be the simplest step in tailoring your relationship. In order to get the relationship between you and your daughter to fit, it is imperative that you take responsibility for and ownership of your "purchase".

We have all had that one dress that we just couldn't leave in the store and had to have! Then, once we got it home, we made sure to hang it up to keep it wrinkle and stain-free – all because we valued it. Just like that dress, your daughter wants to feel valued by you. She wants to feel empowered and that her life has added value to yours and to the world. Believe me, my daughter has an imaginary head the size of a pumpkin because when I owned the fact that I made the decision to have her, I started bragging on her, and to this very day, my bragging has not changed. As excited as you would be about the dress purchase, your daughter would love to hear you give her the assurance that matters most...that you love and value her. In the upcoming chapters, I will suggest some ways that may be helpful to you in making your daughter feel valued.

After we have worn an article quite a few times, we begin to value it less and start overlooking or mishandling it. Have you ever thought that your daughter may feel overlooked or mishandled? When the days of "goo-goo ga-ga" are over and she can feed, bathe, clothe, and entertain herself, it is not the time to disengage from her.

That is the time to start developing the woman you want her to become in the world. I'm sure we all want our daughters to be better than we are (as I tell my daughter all the time). Therefore, as your daughter gets older, consider taking memorable trips with her, having intellectual conversations with her, sharing your past lessons learned, all while reminding her of how valuable she is. I am overwhelmed with gratitude when my adult daughter tells me that the conversations we've had and the wisdom I shared with her made me a great mom in her eyes and the woman she is today.

It's important to note that the most critical time in your daughter's life that she will need her mom is *"always."* It's not unlike the dress you purchased. If you continue to overlook it, and it remains unworn, eventually, you will begin to mishandle it because it has lost its value to you. You become overfamiliar with it because you have allowed newer things to take its place. I do not believe that there's a daughter on Earth who wants to feel rejected by her mom; therefore, after you have made the decision to "purchase" her, you must put forth every effort to nurture her, ensuring she does not feel like a dress in a closet being overlooked, unworn, or mishandled.

You do not ever want her to feel like you both have outgrown the relationship or become less interested in it and not give it any care.

Techniques to Remember

1. In order to get the relationship between you and your daughter to fit, it is imperative that you take responsibility for and ownership of your "purchase".

2. When the days of "goo-goo ga-ga" are over and she can feed, bathe, clothe, and entertain herself, it is not the time to disengage from her.

3. You must put forth every effort to nurture her, ensuring she does not feel like a dress in a closet being overlooked, unworn, or mishandled.

My *Tailoring* Goals

Chapter
TWO

Recognize That
You
Could Fit Better

As I told you already, the first rule of dressing fabulously is making sure your clothes fit well. There are many things that can cause a relationship not to fit properly, and there have been times that my daughter and I did not fit well. If you have not experienced the "ill-fitting" yet, just hold on, look out, and prepare for the ride.

First of all, in order to recognize that your relationship does not fit properly, one of you must stop being in denial! Before social media was prevalent, I watched so many families put on hypocritical acts in public. Social media has taken this to the highest level of deceit thus far. I see mothers and daughters who do not have healthy relationships and who barely like each other post things on social media just to compete with others who may appear to have something authentic. You know, it can be seen like spousal relationships.

All because the "Marriage Challenge" is trending on social media, the unhappiest people jump on the bandwagon and begin conjuring up things to say, posting pictures and videos so they can appear to have something that someone else has.

It grieves me to see this. Posting on social media does not prove to the world that you have a healthy relationship. The hundreds of likes that a post receives do not make things better in the relationship. It is my sincere desire to help mend mother-daughter relationships so that what is posted is genuine. Mothers and daughters have to take a hard look and judge themselves as it relates to their relationships and recognize that they could fit better. Some relationships, like my dress, will need more alterations than others, but together you and your daughter can strive to have a healthy, long-lasting relationship.

Moms, we must first recognize that we can fit better. As much as we may dislike hearing this, I have learned through experience that having the title of mom does not mean that we are always right. At times, I have been flat out wrong and believed I had the right answers when, in fact, I didn't. I have given advice to my daughter out of some of my bad filters. My daughter has plenty of comical stories about how I embarrassed her (and other children) when I felt the need to address certain things. Of course, times like those caused us not to fit well for hours and sometimes days.

Perhaps you have made some decisions that were not so healthy for your mother-daughter relationships, and those decisions brought on tension between the two of you, or perhaps you were not active in your daughter's life, or maybe even though she lived in the house with you, you were "absent" or addicted to alcohol or drugs. Perhaps you abused her physically or mentally or allowed her to be abused. Remember, as the mom, it is your responsibility to be the Lead Tailor in the relationship. Ask your daughter how she thinks the both of you can fit better. It's never too late to acknowledge where you are losing unhealthy weight and begin the tailoring process.

You must be open to your daughter's honesty and know that her perception is her reality. As much as it may hurt, if you are too arrogant to look at vital things that may have caused tension within the relationship, it will take much longer to resolve issues, or you may possibly risk losing the relationship altogether.

Saying that you are sorry and being sincere is the beginning of reconciliation or restoration. Remember that this is the beginning, and it's imperative that you do not sweep the problems under the proverbial rug and want her to just get over a situation all because you apologized – this is the greatest deception. Please know that dust mites will always come back to bite. You will want to address issues within your mother-daughter relationship so that there aren't any hindrances to relationship-building later on. There's more about this in the last chapter.

Depending on the severity of the offense, you and your daughter may need to seek professional help.

While you are reading the next few chapters, ask yourself, "Am I losing unhealthy weight in our relationship?" Your daughter will have to assist in the repair and alterations of the relationship; however, it is ultimately your responsibility to initiate the process. Read on to find out more about how to get your relationship to fit.

Techniques to Remember

1. Ask your daughter how she thinks the both of you can fit better. It's never too late to acknowledge where you are losing unhealthy weight and begin the tailoring process.

2. It's imperative that you do not sweep the problems under the proverbial rug and want her to just get over a situation all because you apologized – this is the greatest deception.

3. Your daughter will have to assist in the repair and alterations of the relationship; however, it is ultimately your responsibility to initiate the process.

My *Tailoring* Goals

_____

_____

_____

_____

_____

_____

_____

_____

_____

_____

_____

_____

_____

_____

_____

_____

_____

_____

_____

_____

_____

Chapter

THREE

Every

Tailor

Possesses a Certain

Skill Set

Now, after we've owned our purchases and we realize that we could fit a bit better within the relationship, there are a few skills that we must possess before we even begin so that we can effectively complete the tailoring process. If you don't take anything else from this book, it's critical that you remember the skill set in this chapter.

The Skill of Patience

This first skill will help you along the way when you feel like giving up. It'll be your friendly reminder that without it, the relationship won't fit. It's the skill that every relationship needs, and it's called Patience! Yes, ma'am, I'm sure your daughter may have given you a very good reason (a time or two) to react first and think later. Maybe you believe that the relationship "is what it is," and there's no hope for it. Well, I want to encourage you to practice this skill so that the tailoring process won't frustrate you.

The best advice I can give regarding this skill is to accept that your daughter is perfectly imperfect, and so are you. Just as much as you need to possess this skill, you might be surprised by how much she may already possess it with you.

Not one of us is perfect, so we must come to the conclusion that we are real people, and this is real life. Your daughter isn't exempt from having feelings and life challenges. You must understand that at times, she is learning to manage her emotions, too. The unique thing about our daughters is that they are young and inexperienced. That is why employing patience is so essential. Our daughters are counting on our gifts of maturity and experience to teach them how to function and navigate through life.

Despite the fact that we live in a "microwave" culture, we must understand that there is no such thing as an automatic relationship. Conventional ovens still exist for a reason. Great relationships are going to take some time and patience to properly prepare.

The Skill of Focus & Intentionality

Relationships that last long are created by a high level of focus and intentionality. I believe that this was one of my greatest skills as a mother. I made a commitment to have an improved relationship with my daughter. Whether you were fortunate enough to have had a great model for a healthy mother-daughter relationship or not, every generation of motherhood should strive to improve, but this takes focus and intentionality.

Set your relationship desires and goals, create a plan, and focus so that you intentionally accomplish them. This skill requires effort. How bad do you want the relationship between you and your daughter to fit well? The following chapters are based on the desires and goals I set and the focus and intentionality that it took to create a healthy relationship with my daughter.

Read on so that you can create a plan and get focused and intentional about tailoring your relationship.

Techniques to Remember

1. Patience is the first skill that will help you along the way when you feel like giving up. It'll be your friendly reminder that without it, the relationship won't fit.

2. Accept that your daughter is perfectly imperfect, and so are you.

3. Set your relationship desires and goals, create a plan, and focus so that you intentionally accomplish them. This skill requires effort.

My *Tailoring* Goals

Chapter FOUR

Training with *Tools* of the Trade

I know this may be a bit of a sensitive area, but the questions I'm about to ask could save you from many challenges and disappointments as your mother-daughter relationship progresses. What does your lifestyle say about you? What tools of the trade are you training with? You remember that old adage: "The apple does not fall too far from the tree." Is your apple, your tool in this case, a good example of who you want your daughter to become?

I can remember not being an example of a good parent. I was a teen mom, and I wanted to have fun and live life as I did before I got pregnant. When my daughter wasn't with her father, I can remember sometimes leaving her with my mom and sisters just so I could hang out with my friends at the lakefront or out at the club. I attempted to spend quality time with my daughter as often as I could; however, I was a young and immature mother who simply wanted to enjoy life.

When my daughter was four-years-old, I made a conscious decision to "pay now and play later." -- John C. Maxwell. I got a job and began attending college. I started to change and decided that I should sacrifice certain things that I enjoyed doing so that I did not repeat a pattern or become a statistic.

I was determined to have some positive tools of the trade to train with. Moreover, I wanted to ensure that years up the road I would be able to say that I'm happy with the product that I crafted.

The Tool of God

The first tool of the trade that I chose to train with was **God**. Yes, I knew that if I wanted a different outcome, I had to allow someone other than me to lead the way. I can honestly say that this has been the greatest and most influential tool of the trade that I have trained with. Now, there is no specific order for utilizing the tools in your relationship sewing kit which you will utilize as appropriate to tailor your relationship.

Just know that the *first* one that I highly recommend that you have and use in order to properly modify your relationship is God.

The Tool of Self-Control

As I stated earlier, your examples are your tools of the trade that you are training your daughter with. It's imperative that we make use of the tool of self-control as parents. I shared a couple of paragraphs earlier that I would drop my daughter off with my mother and sisters so that I could date or "turn-up". Well, had I continued to do that longer than I had done already, my relationship with my daughter might not have turned out successfully, and one of my trade tools might have been called dropped-off.

I had to learn to set personal boundaries for my daughter's sake as well. I sacrificed the public dating scene. Think about it; if you are extremely active, exposing your daughter to different friendships and relationships, you are creating a problem that may not be an easy fix later. You see, if you want to tailor your relationship with your daughter, you must learn to establish personal boundaries, and be discrete with your dating relationships.

Now, I'm not telling you that you cannot have a life with friends or a significant other. I am merely suggesting that you consider sacrificing being a serial dater and/or "turn-up queen" if you do not want to create a problem later. She's your priority. Remember that you are training your daughter with your tools of your trade. She is always observing your example.

If you train with a tool that seems to show that every boyfriend is going to be your husband, then when it is time for her to date, it's possible that she will repeat that pattern. When you are not happy with her following your techniques and you express your frustration or try to offer wisdom, it is also possible that she will use the tools of your trade against you.

The Tool of Maturity

Maturity is a major tool of the trade as well. Women are powerful beings in the earth, yet we are very emotional, and if we are not emotionally intact, we can be melodramatic and extremely immature.

It is our responsibility as moms to ensure that we do not give our young daughters the chance to even dream of becoming the next drama-filled reality television or social media star. We have to be careful that time spent in her presence is not to watch who is fighting or sleeping with whom, or which B is the Baddest B. When you allow your daughter to become engulfed in certain television shows or extreme social media activity, eventually you will see the evidence in her conforming personality. Most of all, she should never have the perception that you are a drama queen who is always looking for a fight. How does she see you react when her teacher has to address an issue about her behavior or a decline in her grades? Or, when the store clerk makes a mistake?

Unfortunately, female drama is at a pinnacle, and women are not maturing as early as they once did. In previous eras, women were married with children and taking care of the house at sixteen. They had other things to worry about other than the immature things that we deal with today.

Training with the tool of maturity in your relationship can save you a lot of time and heartache later. It can also win your daughter and help her to trust your judgment. If you always remain at least three steps beyond your daughter's maturity level, she will eventually model what maturity looks like. She may be placed in quite a few positions to witness that you are the minority in today's culture if you always remain on the top floor of situations and decision-making and never take the escalator to the basement to address immaturity and pettiness.

As a mother and a daughter, I have learned that our daughters follow our examples more than our advice. What she sees in you is what you will probably get from her in the future. Let your daughter trust you to train her with positive tools of the trade to tailor your relationship. Besides, she will be in your classroom for a very long time.

Techniques to Remember

1. Remember that you are training your daughter with your tools of your trade. She is always observing your example.

2. What she sees in you is what you will probably get from her in the future.

3. Let your daughter trust you to train her with positive tools of the trade to tailor your relationship.

My *Tailoring* Goals

_____
_____
_____
_____
_____
_____
_____
_____
_____
_____
_____
_____
_____
_____
_____
_____
_____
_____
_____
_____
_____
_____
_____

Chapter
FIVE

Thread
Your
Relationship with Love

Thread holds our garments together. If a garment is not sewn with the proper thread, there's the possibility that it will tear, not unlike the relationship between you and your daughter. If you do not thread your relationship with love, it may not withstand the considerable stresses that are put on it.

Often, I reminisce about the day I found out I was having a girl. Although it was not the appropriate time to become a mother because I had just graduated from high school, I was elated to hear that she was going to be a girl. During my pregnancy, I remember talking to her and smiling while I rubbed my stomach. It was love before sight!

Considering that a baby grows and develops in its mother's womb until birth, there is a connection that is formed between the two. Naturally babies come into the world expecting to receive love and affection from their mothers as a result of having been intimately connected to them for nine months. It's no surprise that your daughter desires to feel wanted by you.

Therefore, it is your responsibility as the Lead Tailor to begin the threading process of love to tailor your relationships.

I do understand that some of us did not have situations that modeled what a good, healthy, and loving mother-daughter relationship looked like, but it's never too late to learn and begin. It does not matter if your daughter is 2, 16, or 36, the love of a mother can create lasting memories and establish a new culture that can be life-changing. You have the power to show your daughter what the true definition of love is, no matter your circumstances. Instead of forming a habit of arguing and yelling, consider reaffirming your love for her. Life is short, and so often I hear of people finding out they are sick or are on their death beds, and they have so many regrets about not having reconciled relationships.

If you are currently estranged from your daughter, do not allow a devastating moment in life to catch you and cause you to have to live with the regret of not sharing and expressing love for her.

If you properly thread your relationship with love, there is nothing that can easily rip you two apart. Let's get ready to tailor your relationship and sew what is needed to keep the thread of love in place and the garment of your relationship tightly woven.

Techniques to Remember

1. If you do not thread your relationship with love, it may not withstand the considerable stresses that are put on it.

2. You have the power to show your daughter what the true definition of love is, no matter your circumstances.

3. If you are currently estranged from your daughter, do not allow a devastating moment in life to catch you and cause you to have to live with the regret of not sharing and expressing love for her.

My *Tailoring* Goals

Chapter SIX

Watch What You Sew

Now that you have gotten your thread of love in place, it's time to sew and begin repairs and alterations on the relationship. At times, we sew things in our relationships with our daughters that can strain the relationship. What do you want to sew your relationship with? Let's focus on the positive things to sew and help tailor your relationship.

Sew Attention

Can you honestly say that you know who your daughter's teachers and friends are? How often she's on social media? Whether or not she's completed her assignments at school? Society has caused us to detach from what matters most, and that is our emotional attachment with our families and close friends. We have become preoccupied with the digital age, being popular, and keeping up with other people's business. If we took the time to sew our relationships with attention, there's nothing that could come between healthy mother-daughter relationships.

If we created a culture early on of attentiveness in our daughters' lives, they would become accustomed to our being involved in their lives. We must visit and volunteer at our daughters' schools so that we can create a culture where our daughters see that we are engaged. It is crucial that we get to know their friends, and invite them over to the house. Paying attention to what they like and dislike is yet another factor in sewing together a great relationship.

Sew Affection

Affection is "a tender attachment or fondness," and can be expressed by words of tenderness or appropriate, loving, physical touch (Merriam-Webster Dictionary). This piece of thread is extremely valuable. Our daughters need affection from us just as every human needs food and water. Think about it: when we do not eat, we get "hangry". When we do not drink water, we become thirsty and dehydrated. It follows that receiving affection is a necessity for our daughters.

Don't you remember when the touch and smell of your skin comforted her as a baby? Affectionate moments are perfect trust-building opportunities and offer a safe haven in the relationship. Although the means by which she will desire affection may differ as she matures, she will never want to be without it. I have witnessed and heard stories of moms who did not make time or perhaps did not know how to take advantage of some of the most critical, intimate moments with their young daughters.

As their daughters matured, the moms wanted to make up for those lost opportunities, but it was not received well by the daughters. If your daughter was not accustomed to your showing her a considerable amount of affection at five-years-old, do not be surprised if she does not want to be "babied" at age 17. So if you are a mom with a young daughter, take advantage of sewing affection now so that it's not uncomfortable for her later. If your daughter is older, and you missed the beginning stages of bonding with her through showing affection, find out what she is comfortable with now. It's important to know your boundaries so that you do not get your feelings hurt and feel rejected if you are considered a bit extreme or intolerable in her opinion. And no matter what, if she is a teenager or older, be sure not to take it personal. Simply try other means, such as, expressions through cards, giving her a listening ear, words of affirmation, or a simple "I love you."

Sewing affection never gets old, and there are various ways of expressing it. As a matter of fact, my daughter is a young adult, and because I sewed affection consistently, she allows me to show her as much affection as I desire. In most cases, she initiates the act of affection. Often, when we're together, she will grab my hand while we're walking. Sometimes I think it's a bit much, but hey, if she likes it, I love it. She certainly is not ashamed of expressing her affection toward me in public or private.

Sew Sacrifice & Time

Our daughters come in the world by way of our sacrificing through the nine months and the labor pains of delivery. It does not stop there though. If you are adamant about tailoring your relationship with your daughter, you must be willing to sew some additional pieces of the thread of sacrifice and time. Our bodies go through changes, our schedules are adjusted, our personal spending budget changes, and there is so much that is required of us as mothers. Although we are strong, it is not always easy to continue to sew this piece of thread.

In this step, I want to encourage you to line your time up accordingly so that you can defeat weakness within the relationship. Oftentimes, mothers use money to compensate for the lack of effort to express genuine love. Money cannot look into your daughter's eyes and gaze back at her to tell her how much you love her, only you can do that. It takes balance, and that is why you have to line up your investment with time and money.

It's unhealthy to use money to silence your emotional, mental, or physical absence from her life. I have witnessed too many relationships fail for this very reason.

Planning to spend time with your daughter is essential to having a tailor-made relationship. Just as we plan to go to work, date, and other things, it is important that we plan to spend time with our daughters. While she is young, she will require more of your time than she will when she gets older and becomes more involved in extra-curricular activities, work, and dating. Nonetheless, no matter her age, she will value the time and effort that you give her. Plan a tea party or picnic with her, allow her to help you cook a meal, or simply give her your time in a conversation without the distractions of an electronic device.

As she gets older she may not want to hang out as long, but a simple chat over lunch/dinner or even embarrassing her at karaoke night can go a long way. You may not have much money, but the time you spend with her is priceless. Just remember that the reward for moms who sew sacrifice and time for their children is ultimately the greatest.

Sew Money

In addition to time, if you can take a portion of your money and allow your daughter to witness you sacrificing some of it for her needs and some of her wants, it's an additive. Just know that most times, it's engrained in our children that M.O.M. is the acronym for Made of Money – at least that's what my child thinks. She must see that the money you have is not all about your buying nice clothes, shoes, and fine jewelry for yourself and leaving her to look less than well put together. It's sad when I see a mother who has expensive hair extensions and the latest designer clothes and bags yet her child is walking around with a saggy diaper, a dingy onesie and shoes that barely fit. A tailor-made mom ensures that her child receives the basic necessities and the child's appearance looks better than hers.

Furthermore, it does not stop at material things. I'm talking about a good education, extra-curricular activities, orthodontic care if necessary, a savings account, and more if she can afford to do those things. What and who we spend our money on says a lot about us.

Just for the record, sewing your money does not mean spoiling your daughter. As your daughter gets older, things become more expensive because of her size and her taste/desires; therefore, I am a firm believer that after basic necessities, she should be rewarded for good grades and behavior. Otherwise, she should work and earn her own money for the additional things that she desires to have. As a mom, it is important that you invest properly so that you do not look up and regret investing money into a rebellious child who has not put any effort into honoring you as her parent and preparing for a bright future. You must know how to set limitations with how you invest your money in your child.

Sew Confidence

I often talk to young mothers to encourage them to gain influence with their daughters before the school teacher or counselor does. In my dialog, I use the analogy of the movie The Help where the housekeeper continuously told the little girl, "You is smart; you is kind; you is important." Although the housekeeper built the little girl's esteem, her mother missed the opportunity.

In this movie, some of the housekeepers had more influence with the children than the mothers. I could not imagine Monaye responding to someone other than me as those children responded in the movie. If I did not tell her who she was, I would have been giving someone else the needle to thread something other than what I wanted.

I tailored my relationship with my daughter by affirming her daily. I can remember when she was a baby I created songs about how pretty and smart she was. I knew that she desired to be accepted by me and needed my affirmation to build her confidence. As a matter of fact, at times, I used to believe that my affirmation caused her to become narcissistic, but then I asked myself whether I would have preferred her to lack confidence and have self-esteem issues or know who she is and have to teach her humility.

Communicating *positive* words to your daughter gives her the courage to fight off negative words spoken to her by others and builds her confidence. Social media, television, and cultural pressures give such a superficial definition of what beauty is. Unfortunately, it can cause our daughters to compare themselves to what is presented as beautifully accepted. As moms, it's important that we diligently create an environment and have a voice that speaks to her confidence. If we aren't careful, our daughters could possibly begin to hurt themselves in unimaginable ways just to fit how society tells them they should be. They must know that it's not skin color, weight, hair texture, clothes or shoes, or even a socio-economic status that defines them. It is a cultural battle that moms must combat early and never stop.

It is not the responsibility of the neighbor, the school teacher, mentor, preacher, or anyone else to tell your daughter how great she is. Those people should only confirm what you have already said. There is nothing like a mother who knows how to esteem her daughter and tell her that her life has meaning. You have the power to thread confidence and affirm your daughter. If you practice this often, she will always trust that you will tell her who she really is and is becoming – a queen, a princess, pretty, adorable, intelligent, kind, a world changer, a leader, etc.

Sew Purpose

The late Mr. Ned Odum used to say, "When you've said it to them once, say it again, and again, and again." I can remember some of the things that our village constantly said to my daughter that became ingrained in her mind. "You're a star. You have purpose. Remember who you are. You're not like everyone else. You were born to be great.

You're a leader, not a follower. Think BIG. Think, think, think for yourself." These words were the driving force, sewing purpose in her.

Often, daughters grow up not realizing the potential that they possess to offer the world until late into their adulthood. It's our obligation to sew purpose so that she'll know that her life doesn't have to be lived by happenstance. If we sew purpose and expose her to positive things, her ambition will not be to become an overnight social media success star known for negative things that invite a particular audience. You don't want her to live needing the approval of and negative attention from the world.

We must get involved in our daughters' lives and keep them busy doing productive things so that they will know that their lives have a greater piece of thread holding them together. It's called purpose. It is imperative that you keep your daughter active with meaningful activities that stimulate her mind, stir her gift, build her confidence, expose her to a diverse group of people, and surround her with positive influences. Keep her busy so that she is too tired to be involved in things that do not serve a purpose for where she is going in life. It's never too early to teach her that she must resist the temptations that will come to sabotage her purpose.

Based on my experience, in addition to ingraining phrases in her brain early on, the best way to teach her is to show her that you are living your own life purposefully. Sophia Nelson said, "We are defined early on by our families, the first place we learn how to be, and what to be." I'm not saying that I did not make a few unwise choices, but I mostly made sure that I rarely took days off work and brought her to my job to see me use my gift and serve my purpose. I also ensured that we consistently served our community through volunteering for programs, and later on we established a business together. It was important for me to show her that her life has a purpose and that she could choose to make every day count toward fulfilling it.

So moms, you must always remember that you are tailoring the relationship, and if she witnesses a pattern of your being mature, making things happen with confidence, passion, and purpose, she will desire to emulate that. Remember, what I said in the previous chapter, your daughter will follow your example more than she will listen to your words. Sew purpose.

Sew Effective Communication

Effective communication is such a valuable piece of thread in the tailoring process. When people visit a tailor, they must properly communicate what their feelings are about the garment and what they need from the tailor. It's no different in a mother-daughter relationship. This was another area of my mother-daughter relationship that I had to grow in. If you want to save your relationship from quite a few challenges, the both of you must utilize effective communication.

The first part of this challenge is to know how to be present in the conversation. Often, we have cellphones, computers, televisions, and other things that cause us to be distracted when one or the other is communicating. This can cause a problem when it's time to remember what you or she may have said. Not being present also has the potential to place a barrier between the two of you if neither of you feels the other is being attentive.

Next, we must know that we have the power to guide the communication. We cannot have a history of being abrasive and expect a good response from our daughters. Neither can we have a history of being passive and expect a good outcome in certain situations. It's important that we know how to communicate what our expectations of her are and what consequences may follow if she consistently fails to meet those expectations.

In addition to the aforementioned, moms should always consider that listening is a gift and an extremely valuable piece of the thread of effective communication. This was extremely challenging for me. I look back and laugh at myself about a lot of my failures to listen. I'd developed a reputation that I had an answer or knew what she was thinking before she could finish a sentence or her story. As she got older, and I intentionally began to practice listening, she was able to successfully communicate her thoughts, stories, and feelings. I was happy that I learned to ask questions and to understand her thinking. If I hadn't learned to do this early, I may have had to live with the regret of my daughter having given someone else the privilege of listening to her.

I'll talk more about another method of effective communication later in the Know When to Taper Your Mouth chapter.

Techniques to Remember

1. It's unhealthy to use money to silence your emotional, mental, or physical absence from her life.

2. It is imperative that you keep your daughter active with meaningful activities that stimulate her mind, stir her gift, build her confidence, expose her to a diverse group of people, and surround her with positive influences.

3. We cannot have a history of being abrasive and expect a good response from our daughters. Neither can we have a history of being passive and expect a good outcome in certain situations.

My *Tailoring* Goals

Chapter
SEVEN

Fuse
Honesty
&
Transparency

There are times when tailoring requires two different materials to be fused or joined together. This part of the sewing technique can be a bit tricky, but it's one that is extremely essential if you are trying to get your mother-daughter relationship to fit. The two things I recommend being joined are honesty and transparency. Without honesty and transparency, the relationship can lock up and not function properly. Exactly the same thing is possible with a sewing machine when the technique is not used properly.

If we want to win our daughters and hope that they will be honest with us, we can't always take an intimidating posture. All of us may have [at one time or another] failed at this. Sometimes we lack the patience and wisdom to understand that her openness and honesty enhance the relationship. It creates an opportunity for us as moms to become even more influential.

We have to intentionally break down barriers so that our daughters do not always feel intimidated by our responses. Although it may be challenging, we have to understand that it is not always appropriate to condemn, discipline, or lecture her two seconds into her vulnerability. She does not want to feel judged or humiliated by you. Our daughters face a lot of difficult things beyond the walls of our homes, and if we do not provide an outlet for them to express things, they may eventually become resentful and close us out. We have the power to cause them to look at things differently, take a different route in a situation, and make them feel like they are capable of doing anything. Those things, though, take skill. Ask her questions. Now, here's the twist to this part of tailoring – it can cause you some sleepless nights and some crying days. It's important, however, that you brace yourself for what you may hear or learn.

For as long as I can remember, my daughter and I have joined honesty and transparency. Again, I wanted what I did not experience in my relationship with my mom. I always told Monaye that she could tell me anything, even if she thought it would make me upset. I made a vow to her that if she trusted me enough to tell me, I would help walk her through anything no matter how much it may hurt her. She also knew that with every decision, there is a consequence, but I needed her to be willing to take the risk with me more than anyone else.

For example, I often talked to Monaye about the risks of having sex prematurely. Although I did not get the talk from my mother growing up, I was determined to share valuable information with her that I wish I could have learned from my mom versus having the experience and listening to my peers. Monaye heard it from me first. We were very appropriately open. Note that I said "appropriately open." Our conversations intensified when she began dating.

By the time she was going off to college, she would always joke and say that when she decided to "do it", she was going to call me on the phone and say, "Mommy, I'm about to have sex. Ok. Love you. I'm sorry. Bye!" and hang up. Of course, that was a joke, but that was her way of saying, I promise that I will tell you. Some of the moms I have had encounters with have said that they do not want to be a part of knowing certain things, and I respect their opinions; however, in my case, the things that my daughter has been honest with me about have helped her make better decisions.

By now, you may be wondering how you should respond to all of this honesty. Well, I took advantage of the opportunity and decided to be transparent with her. Many times, the silence of our past experiences in the lives of our children just ends up creating a culture that repeats unhealthy cycles. It is imperative that we create a culture of transparency so that our daughters can know that no one is perfect, not even their mothers.

I used my wisdom, and my past experiences to initiate conversations so that she would feel comfortable enough to be honest and transparent. At the end of every conversation, I would use my favorite quote by Michael Jordan, "So do not be like me; be better than me." I'm a witness that the culture of honesty and transparency that my daughter and I shared inevitably made me her biggest influence.

Now moms, you may be wondering if I'm saying to expose all of your life history unfiltered to your daughter. NO! Transparency has its limitations. There are some things that aren't intended for our daughters to know because it may not be appropriate to share, or it may not be the right time to share it. I shared some of my past experiences and some of the experiences of others who may have dealt with certain issues. At times I would use Jack or Jill or Mickey or Minnie to talk about real life stories so that she would never know whose experience I was using. I never wanted to expose anyone else, and there were some things that I did in my past that she should believe Jill did, not me.

You may say that's not being honest; however, I have learned through experience that we must use wisdom in all things. You do not ever want to risk your daughter losing respect for you because you did not use wisdom or have a strategy when you shared something with her. Remember I said that the joining process can be very tricky during the tailoring process. Well, so you do not cause your relationship to lock up and not function properly, always remember what you share and how you share it may inadvertently do more harm than good. Be careful when you are joining honesty and transparency.

Techniques to Remember

1. If we want to win our daughters and hope that they will be honest with us, we can't always take an intimidating posture.

2. Although it may be challenging, we have to understand that it is not always appropriate to condemn, discipline, or lecture her two seconds into her vulnerability. She does not want to feel judged or humiliated by you.

3. Many times, the silence of our past experiences in the lives of our children just ends up creating a culture that repeats unhealthy cycles.

My *Tailoring* Goals

_____
_____
_____
_____
_____
_____
_____
_____
_____
_____
_____
_____
_____
_____
_____
_____
_____
_____
_____
_____
_____
_____
_____
_____

Chapter
EIGHT

Know When
to
Taper
Your
Mouth

Some times tailors have to taper pants because the leg of the pants may be too wide/big. Immediately when I realized that I was going to use tapering in this book since it was a part of the tailoring process, the first thing that came to my mind was my *MOUTH*. Have you ever thought that maybe your mouth is too big? Okay, maybe not. Let me ask this then: has your significant other ever alluded to or directly stated that you have a wonderful way of expressing your opinion or reminding him of something that was not done correctly or fast enough?

This part of tailoring my relationship with my daughter was an epic fail on so many levels. I am continuously practicing the art of how to taper my mouth. We all know that a woman's tongue can be a deadly weapon on the right day and at the right moment. Not all of us as moms have mastered putting more sugar than spice on our tongue or when to just be silent. Most of the time we kind of have an idea of what the outcome of a situation is going to be, and it just kills us to not say it so we can have the glory later of saying, "I told you so," especially to our companions and children. Can you remember as a child some of the things that your mom may have said to you that you felt she could have or should have said differently, or you laugh about it now and say she really did not have to go there because she completely overreacted?

At times we can be very controlling, condescending, and irritating in our daughters' lives as they mature into adulthood. We believe that our status gives us permission to go off on her with no filter. Well mom, guess what? That very thing will eventually alienate our daughters, and it may take a long while to win them back.

As our daughters mature into adulthood, we may need to reconsider how we actually say some things or when we should simply taper our mouths, depending on the circumstance. I know you are probably saying, so what, I'm the mother, or I just want the best for my daughter, and of course, you are, and you should. But... as I stated earlier, me and my big mouth have failed at this so tremendously, and I am still a work in progress. It is a learning process, and if we can learn when to taper our mouths at the right time, we may actually succeed at one of the greatest parts of tailoring.

I can remember when my daughter thought she had all the right answers as it relates to dating. Nothing that I or anyone else said to her could convince her that she may have been blinded by her decisions and actions. Quite often during her dating years I attempted to tell her how she should say and do things differently, yet she insisted that I just did not get it. Of course, during those times we did not fit properly, and I didn't know how to taper my mouth.

Most daughters will reach an age and begin to think they have lived life much longer than you. They may actually believe in their own minds that they are more experienced and have an answer for everything. I'm sure you, too, can remember when you told your mom, "but you just don't get it", or thinking to yourself, "She's just old and doesn't understand that we're not living in ancient times". Just as some of our moms may have done, we must know when it's time to simply allow life to run its course so that we do not alienate our daughters, especially if it's ordinary life situations such as infatuation that does not cause serious harm to your daughter.

I decided to challenge myself to only offer advice when asked, and inevitably that helped our relationship to fit better. To sum up the discussion in the most memorable way, we should just know when to make use of the skill of "*shut up*".

Techniques to Remember

1. As our daughters mature into adulthood, we may need to reconsider how we actually say some things or when we should simply taper our mouths, depending on the circumstance.

2. Just as some of our moms may have done, we must know when it's time to simply allow life to run its course so that we do not alienate our daughters, especially if it's ordinary life situations such as infatuation that does not cause serious harm to your daughter.

3. To sum up the discussion in the most memorable way, we should just know when to make use of the skill of "shut up".

My *Tailoring* Goals

Measuring Tapes,
Respect,
and
Boundaries

G ood tailors know that by far one of the most essential things in tailoring is that you have to have measurements. There's no way that you can be a successful tailor without properly measuring the person and the garment so that you will know what work you are doing. Well, when you are tailoring your mother-daughter relationship, it is essential that you use the measuring tape of respect, and set boundaries. This part of the tailoring process can certainly cause tension in the relationship if it is not done. Let me explain.

Have you ever witnessed a mom laughing at her daughter putting her hand on her hip or pointing her finger to express her opinion all while the mother and people around her encourage her to continue? That was me when my daughter was a toddler. I thought it was funny and cute when she would mimic my behavior. She knew how to roll her neck, and do all the above until the day I came to my senses. Unfortunately, this type of behavior seems to be acceptable and quite common now. If you think it is cute for her to be disrespectful at age two and you don't teach her to be respectful early, you will regret it by the time she is twelve. We must establish healthy boundaries and pull out the measuring tapes to ensure that respect or, in some instances, disrespect does not cause our relationships to be tailored improperly.

We must never allow our daughters to become too comfortable with us and assume that they are our girlfriends, sisters, or anything else before we are their mothers. I have watched and heard of so many mothers who did not establish healthy boundaries. They condoned underage drinking, smoking, premature dating, sex in their homes, etc., and they had no idea that they were creating an environment for dishonor.

There is a saying, *"Good fences make good neighbors."* Mothers should always be the leaders and set boundaries so that daughters know not to go beyond the fence. Our daughters are not our best friends though it is possible that we are hers. It is unhealthy if she is your best friend. Healthy mothers have healthy relationships with their own peers. You should not need to look to your daughter to be your friend. You do not want to miss using the measuring tape for respect. Be careful that you do not strive to be more of her friend and end up destroying the relationship because of dishonor.

You must set boundaries so that your relationship does not tear apart in the tailoring process. I can remember while my daughter was growing up, some of our family members and acquaintances would whisper that I was strict. I don't necessarily agree with the word strict; however, I would define my method as firmly fair. While the naysayers were whispering, I was setting standards. My daughter didn't understand that not only was I using the measuring tape of respect and boundaries to parent her, those measuring skills would subsequently be beneficial to her future.

You must set a precedence that will silently remind her that you are producing greatness, and you can't successfully accomplish that without setting boundaries. It is hard being too liberal in a relationship, allowing anything to go and later wanting to "put your foot down" and command that she change her ways…hard.

I have witnessed this too often in mother-daughter relationships. If you believe that your relationship may be challenged in this area because you did not pull out the measuring tape earlier, talk to your daughter. If you have already created a liberal environment and she is not willing to change, then maybe the two of you should consider speaking to a licensed professional to work it out.

1. We must establish healthy boundaries and pull out the measuring tapes to ensure that respect or, in some instances, disrespect does not cause our relationships to be tailored improperly.

2. You do not want to miss using the measuring tape for respect. Be careful that you do not strive to be more of her friend and end up destroying the relationship because of dishonor.

3. You must set a precedence that will silently remind her that you are producing greatness, and you can't successfully accomplish that without setting boundaries.

My *Tailoring* Goals

Chapter
TEN

There Will Come a
Time When
You'll
Have to… Cut It Off

As you can see by now, tailors use a range of tools, and they all have a purpose. Some of those tools are designed for cutting. The purpose of this section is to protect your daughter. As moms, we sometimes know when some things and people are not worthy of being in our lives, and we get enough courage to cut them off. At other times, we choose to hold on to them and ignore every sign because of an unmet need or for other unhealthy reasons. It is our job to always look at the bigger picture and know when it's time to use the cutting tools to eliminate people from our circle who are not beneficial to us and who are unhealthy to us or our daughters. We should be very cautious of who we expose our daughters to. Part of our responsibility is to protect her from relatives, friends, and neighbors who may not be good for her environment.

Put your antennas up! Be cautious and protective. Do not become so comfortable that you lack wisdom when leaving her with various people (men or women) – even some family members. It only takes one wrong decision to alter our daughter's entire life through molestation, physical abuse, etc. She is counting on you to protect her. As she grows older, she will be happy that her Lead Tailor used cutting tools and did not allow certain types of people to be active in her life. This can be difficult, yet it is extremely beneficial.

In addition to using the cutting tools to eliminate certain people from our circle, we may also have to consider cutting off certain places. I can remember when I made one of the most heartbreaking decisions in the history of my existence. I left the first and only city that I knew and loved. Despite how some people felt about Chicago, it was my city. It was where my family, friends, and social life brought me comfort, happiness, and excitement.

Chicago taught me survival skills to prepare me for my future. Although I knew the world was bigger, I never imagined actually living hundreds of miles away from the place that helped make me the individual that I had become. While this part of the tailoring process was merely intended to cut off Chicago, this sharp tool stabbed me. I was emotionally attached to my city, and detaching from it was painful. The pain from this stab wound continued for almost five years before I accepted that there was a plan and a purpose for the cutting tool.

It never occurred to me that moving to Georgia would help tailor my relationship with my daughter. In addition to our relationship, it was the driving force to create another culture for her, and it gave her experiences and opportunities that she may have never been afforded otherwise. As I reflect on my bittersweet relocation, I understand why I had to use the cutting tool and cut off my place of comfort.

Now, I'm not necessarily saying that you need to cut off a physical city, but perhaps you should ask yourself if there is a place that you frequent that may not be healthy for you or a place that you allow your daughter to go that may expose her to unhealthy or unsafe activities as we discussed earlier in this chapter. As moms, we must use this essential cutting tool... by any means necessary.

1. We should be very cautious of who we expose our daughters to. Part of our responsibility is to protect her from relatives, friends, and neighbors who may not be good for her environment. Put your antennas up! Be cautious and protective.

2. In addition to using the cutting tools to eliminate certain people from our circle, we may also have to consider cutting off certain places.

3. Ask yourself if there is a place that you frequent that may not be healthy for you or a place that you allow your daughter to go that may expose her to unhealthy or unsafe activities.

My *Tailoring* Goals

_____

_____

_____

_____

_____

_____

_____

_____

_____

_____

_____

_____

_____

_____

_____

_____

_____

_____

_____

_____

_____

_____

Chapter
ELEVEN

Double-Back & Reinforce: Do Not Let *Your* Relationship Unravel

During the tailoring process, it's very important that you reinforce a smaller or looser stitch to make it stronger. If you want to make your relationship with your daughter fit even better and not unravel, you must use the double-back and reinforce technique. I recommend that you add a few stiches to some of the aforementioned techniques. We all know that when we think we have done just about everything right, one or two things that were not maintained or sewn correctly at the time of tailoring the relationship can later cause the seams of the "garment" to begin unraveling.

Get Reacquainted with Her

We must know how to handle our daughters differently. Tailors have to learn the use of various settings on each sewing machine – when different needles and thread types should be used. For example, I can remember several times that I had to double-back with my daughter. It's funny when I think about how I never put black pepper on her food when she was a child and even as a teenager because she never liked the taste of it. Well, once when she came home from college to visit, I made dinner that included a baked potato, and I did not put any pepper on it. While we were preparing to eat together, I noticed that she got up from the table and went to the cabinet to get the black pepper to put on her potato. I was shocked and asked her what she was doing. Now, I was extremely curious to know when she started eating black pepper on her food. You won't believe the answer she gave me. Actually, she answered my question with a question. She asked me, "When did I not eat black pepper on my food?" She did not even remember not liking black pepper. The nerve of her! But then I had an epiphany... I needed to double-back and get new information so I could learn about the new Monaye.

As your daughter matures into adulthood, she's going to outgrow being the little girl who you once held in your arms. Your relationship will begin to change, but if you have tailored it appropriately, her changing will not be for the worse. It is vital that you evolve with your daughter to continue to enhance your relationship. It's similar to getting your tailor-made dress dry cleaned in order to keep it maintained. You need to ask questions, and pay attention to the responses.

Ask for Forgiveness

I know you're probably thinking, "Who? Forgive who?!" I'm sure there have been more times than you probably want to count that you wanted your daughter to ask you to forgive her. I completely understand! Writing about that would require me to do another book, so in this chapter, we're going to talk to the mature party – you. Often, as adults, we have difficulty asking our children to forgive us because we don't usually think that it's necessary. We must always find a way to double-back and see if we could have possibly done or said something differently to our daughters. Have you ever thought to ask your daughter if there is something, or do you already know of something that one of you placed in the back of your mind's closet to bury that may need to be addressed now in your mother-daughter relationship?

We must start asking hard questions and be open to our daughters' honest answers about offenses. Perhaps you were very aggressive to the point of abuse with your responses because of your stress level. Or maybe you were tired of feeling alone and were depressed so you did not spend a lot of time with her. No matter what the situation was that may have put some sort of strain on your relationship, when your daughter brings the offense to your attention, be open to listen without interruptions and without being defensive. Consider being sensitive to her feelings so that you can acknowledge that her feelings are real. It takes a lot of humility to admit when we are wrong and to ask our children for forgiveness.

I have known of mothers who were aware that their daughters were being molested by the mothers' husbands, boyfriends, or family members, and they preferred that the daughters keep it a secret. In a few cases the daughters obeyed the mother, held the secret with hatred toward the mother, and the pain of it drove the daughter to drugs and/or suicide and other self-destructive things. In cases of such deep secrets, simply saying, "I'm sorry" is not enough. Too often, we want to just stop there, but professional help by a licensed specialist is highly recommended. No one should be embarrassed about seeking therapy. It is unfair to your daughter for her to have to hold on to things that may be driving her to be something or someone she was never meant to be. Again, merely talking about it between the two of you may not be enough. Do not be ashamed to find a good counselor who can assist you in dealing with deeply-rooted issues.

So, whether great or small, be sure to always double-back to ensure that your relationships do not unravel.

.

Techniques to Remember

1. Your relationship will begin to make changes, but if you have tailored it appropriately, her changing will not be for the worse. It is vital that you evolve with your daughter to continue to enhance your relationship.

2. No matter what the situation was that may have put some sort of strain on your relationship, when your daughter brings the offense to your attention, be open to listen without interruptions and without being defensive.

3. Do not be ashamed to find a good counselor who can assist you in dealing with deeply-rooted issues.

My *Tailoring* Goals

_____

_____

_____

_____

_____

_____

_____

_____

_____

_____

_____

_____

_____

_____

_____

_____

_____

_____

_____

_____

_____

_____

_____

_____

_____

Chapter TWELVE

Put The *Finishing* Touches On It

Probably the most difficult and emotional part of the tailoring process is putting the finishing touches on your tailor-made relationship. Yes, what you have put together fits well, and you may be excited to wear it, but now you will have to trust that every stitch you put in place will achieve the look you desire and hold until the end. Inevitably, there will come a time when you will have to let go and trust that primary tool – *God*. Additionally, you will need to hope and believe that what you sewed, joined, and reinforced in your relationship does not "malfunction" as Janet Jackson's outfit did during the Super Bowl.

Now, this is going to hurt you more than it will hurt her probably, but to put the finishing touches on your tailored relationship, you have to understand that one day, being bossy won't be accepted. Instead, you will have to ask questions such as, "Have you considered..." Instead of telling them "This is what you need to do...,"

You may have to allow your daughters to make some decisions that may be unwise so that they can learn from them. Although our opinions should be valued by our daughters, it is quite predictable that there will come a time when they will prefer that we not offer them.

My daughter is an adult woman, with a career, and her own home, and it has been a journey having to trust that what I have imparted to her will work. At times, I have had to talk myself into understanding that it is life that can be her greatest teacher. Even if things do work out in the way she hopes they will, it is up to us as moms to be present and ready to lend an ear when some things do not work out as our daughters dream they will. We must be careful not to use certain situations as opportunities to control and manipulate our daughters or to be cynical.

We must trust that when life throws her a curve ball, she will remember the tools and wisdom you gave her. She may even come to you and seek your advice if you have tailored your relationship just right. Be sure to use those moments to put some of the tools in this book to good use. Remember everything that you invested in the tailoring and be hopeful that she will take advantage of those things to make you proud.

After you have put the finishing touches on your relationship, never forget that you are the Lead Tailor and must attempt to maintain the relationship so that it will function and fit properly. Unfortunately, there is **no "one-size-fits-all"** for tailoring your mother-daughter relationship, but I hope something in this book has helped in some way to aid you in the process. This is just the first step... Best wishes in all your relationship endeavors.

Techniques to Remember

1. Now you will have to trust that every stitch you put in place will achieve the look you desire and hold until the end. Inevitably, there will come a time when you will have to let go and trust that primary tool – God.

2. We must be careful not to use certain situations as opportunities to control and manipulate our daughters or to be cynical.

3. Remember everything that you invested in the tailoring and be hopeful that she will take advantage of those things to make you proud.

My *Tailoring* Goals

_____

_____

_____

_____

_____

_____

_____

_____

_____

_____

_____

_____

_____

_____

_____

_____

_____

_____

_____

_____

_____

_____

Reference

<u>The Help</u> by Kathryn Stockett

Connect with the Author

To invite Morenda to speak at your event, email:

morenda@tailormademom.com
or
made@motheranddaughterenterprise.com

For products and information about how you can partner with Morenda to elevate your mother-daughter relationship, visit:

www.tailormademom.com
or
www.motheranddaughterenterprise.com

tailor_made_mom
mother_and_daughter_enterprise

Tailor-Made Mom
Mother And Daughter Enterprise

Tailor_Made_Mom
MotherAndDaughterEnt